AF669370

About the Authors

Jayakumar K R is a passionate advocate for responsible AI adoption and its transformative potential across industries. With over three decades of experience spanning the evolution from client-server architectures to cloud-based enterprise solutions, he has made significant contributions to global software product development and deployment.

Having worked with leading organizations such as Bhaba Atomic Research Center, Tata Institute of Fundamental Research, Best & Crompton, and Ramco Systems, Jayakumar later founded Amitysoft Technologies, which delivers ERP and AI products and services to enterprises.

An early champion of software quality assurance, testing, and measurement, he pioneered innovative career paths in software quality and governance. Beginning his career in mainframe systems operations and programming at renowned computing research centres, Jayakumar brings both technical depth and strategic foresight to his work. He currently serves on the International Advisory Council of COSMIC—the Common Software Measurement International Consortium—where he leads the AI Task Force on *Managing Innovative AI Projects*.

Jayakumar holds a Ph.D. from École de Technologie Supérieure – University of Quebec (Canada), along with several professional certifications. Deeply committed to mentoring students and emerging professionals, and an avid writer, he shares his insights regularly through his WordPress blog, blending thought leadership with practical guidance.

Prof. Alain Abran is an Emeritus Professor at École de Technologie Supérieure (ETS), University of Quebec (Canada). Before entering

academia, he spent 20 years in the industry, contributing to information systems development and gaining deep practical experience. He has since devoted over two decades to teaching and research, becoming a pioneering figure in software engineering, particularly in software measurements.

He is a co-inventor of the COSMIC Function Point method—an advanced approach to functional size measurement that has been recognized as an international ISO standard. He played a foundational role in establishing COSMIC (Common Software Measurement International Consortium), where he continues to contribute in various capacities.

He has published extensively in leading academic journals and has guided numerous international research initiatives. Prof. Abran served as executive co-editor of the *Guide to the Software Engineering Body of Knowledge (SWEBOK)* (www.swebok.org), a globally recognized reference in the field. He is also the author of a number of books: *Software Project Estimation* and *Software Metrics & Software Metrology* , Software Maintenance Management: Evaluation & Continuous Improvements (all published by Wiley) and *COSMIC Function Points: Theory & Advanced Practices* (published by CRC Press).

Prof. Abran's work continues to shape the global discourse on software engineering and AI project management, and his contributions remain a cornerstone for practitioners and researchers alike.

Managing Innovative AI Projects
Authors: Jayakumar K R and Alain Abran

This book is a work of non-fiction. The views, strategies, and practices presented herein are those of the authors. While every effort has been made to ensure accuracy, the authors and publisher make no representations or warranties regarding the completeness, reliability, or suitability of the content. The reader is responsible for applying judgment when using the material in real-world situations.

Disclaimer

The content of this book is provided for informational and educational purposes only. It does not constitute professional advice in project management, artificial intelligence, business, legal, financial, or regulatory matters. The authors and publisher expressly disclaim any liability for any direct or indirect damages, losses, or consequences arising from the use, application, or interpretation of the material contained herein. Readers should consult qualified professionals before making decisions based on the content of this book.

First Edition

ISBN: **978-93-344-1940-5**

Cover Design: Generated with the assistance of OpenAI's ChatGPT
For permissions or inquiries please contact: jayakumar@aol.in
Self-Published by: Jayakumar K R

Managing Innovative AI Projects

The Imperative for

AI Specific

Project Management

Jayakumar K R
Alain Abran

Contents

Acknowledgements

This book, Managing Innovative AI Projects, would not have been possible without the invaluable support, encouragement, and inspiration of mentors, colleagues, collaborators, and loved ones who have walked alongside me throughout this journey.

I am deeply thankful to Professor Alain Abran, my co-author and long-time mentor, whose enduring encouragement and thoughtful guidance have shaped the trajectory of my research and professional journey. His intellectual generosity and countless suggestions throughout the development of this book have enriched its clarity, depth, and relevance.

I also extend my sincere thanks to Professor Pierre Bourque, Department of Software Engineering and IT, for his steadfast support and belief in our mission. His vision and quiet strength lent legitimacy and momentum to the completion of this work.

Special appreciation is due to Dr. Ali Idri, the AI Task Force leader, whose strategic direction and the insightful webinars he curated provided a rich foundation for refining this book. The discussions and feedback from that session were instrumental in sharpening its focus and relevance. To all core members and contributors of the AI Task Force—your commitment, wisdom, and camaraderie have been deeply inspiring and are reflected in every page.

I'm truly thankful to my colleagues and team members whose collaboration across real-world AI projects shaped the insights shared in this book. I also benefitted from the wider network of technical professionals whose experiences, perspectives, and generous inputs enriched my understanding. These collective learnings helped me distil complex realities into practical, accessible guidelines—offered here for the benefit of the larger community.

Beyond professional collaborations, I owe a special debt to those who have stood by me personally—especially my life partner, Kalpana, whose love, patience, and quiet resilience sustained me through the turbulent times we faced. Her unwavering support gave me the strength to persevere and the space to create.

To my family and close friends, thank you for your encouragement and understanding as I took up the challenge of writing on the evolving landscape of Information Technology. Your belief in me—often unspoken but always felt—was a source of quiet motivation and strength. I hope this work reflects the values and aspirations we share.

I deeply appreciate the many unnamed individuals—teachers, peers, reviewers, and readers— all who have contributed directly or indirectly to this endeavour, I remain sincerely thankful.

Jayakumar K R

Preface

The discourse on Artificial Intelligence has exploded beyond the labs of technologists and into the boardrooms of every industry. Executives, policymakers, and scholars are captivated by its transformative potential, yet equally wary of its perils: inherent biases, unsettling hallucinations, and profound societal disruption.

In this climate of immense promise and equally enormous risk, organizations are investing billions into AI initiatives. However, behind the headlines, a sobering reality persists: a significant majority of these AI projects fail. They stumble not necessarily due to flawed algorithms, but due to a familiar pitfall— poor project management, now magnified by AI's unique complexities. These are not conventional software projects; they are exploratory, data-hungry, and ethically fraught, demanding a new managerial playbook.

This book, therefore, is not about the intricacies of neural networks or large language models or even project management theory. It is an urgent field guide for the seasoned project manager and the business leader tasked with shepherding these innovative ventures to success.

Drawing on decades of experience in software project metrics and management, we provide a structured framework to de-risk the AI journey. Inside, you will find:

- A breakdown of distinct AI project development phases and their unique challenges.
- A tailored analysis of AI-specific risks, from data acquisition nightmares to model drift in production.
- Practical strategies for tailoring project life cycle based on project type.
- A recommended set of Key Performance Indicators (KPIs) designed to provide visibility and maintain control from conception to value realization.

The message is clear: success in AI cannot be delegated to the data science team alone. It is earned through disciplined management vision, rigorous planning, adaptive monitoring, and deliberate deployment. This book provides the concepts and techniques to do exactly that—to not just adopt AI, but to adapt and deliver it successfully, reaping its profound benefits while mitigating its potential dangers.

Alain Abran

1.0 The Imperative for AI-Specific Project Management

Artificial Intelligence has transcended hype to become a core driver of competitive advantage, with innovations spanning predictive analytics, generative systems, and autonomous agents. Yet, traditional project management frameworks fail to address AI's unique complexities: *probabilistic outputs*, *ethical minefields*, and *dynamic technical dependencies*. This book bridges that gap—providing actionable strategies to navigate uncertainty while delivering measurable value. They equip leaders to transform AI's potential into *responsible, scalable outcomes* by harmonizing innovation ambition with operational discipline.

1.1 Scope and Structure

This book synthesizes proven methodologies with emerging best practices across five critical dimensions:

1. **Project Typology**: Classifies initiatives from *incremental* optimizations to *disruptive* breakthroughs enabling targeted resource allocation.
2. **Adaptive Lifecycles**: Introduces a rigor-scaled AI Project Life Cycle (APLC) that flexes to project risk profiles.
3. **Risk Mitigation**: Systematically addresses technical, ethical, operational, and stakeholder risks through proactive safeguards.
4. **Performance Governance**: Establishes Technical/ Business/ Operational/Ethical KPIs to quantitatively track progress and ROI.
5. **Execution Toolkits**: Provides phase-specific tasks, typical metrics, and tool recommendations for real-world implementation.

1.2 Intended Audience & Application

Designed for:

- **Project Leaders** scaling AI pilots to production.
- **Technical Teams** navigating model development trade-offs.

- **Executives** overseeing AI strategy and investment.
- **Compliance Officers** ensuring ethical alignment.

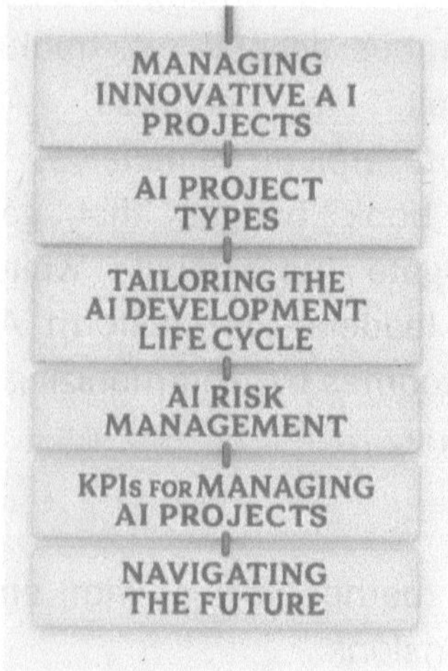

Figure 1.1 Scope of the Book

1.3 What this is not

These guidelines are not:

- A comprehensive or theoretical treatment of general project management principles.
- A reference manual that rehashes foundational PM processes, templates, or methodologies you have already mastered.
- A deep dive into AI algorithms, data science techniques, or software engineering best practices.

Instead, these guidelines:

- Enable seasoned project managers to adopt, adapt, and deliver AI projects rapidly.
- Provide a process-driven approach to integrate a tailored AI Project Life Cycle (APLC) into your existing workflows.
- Highlight only the critical touchpoints, decision gates, and governance mechanisms unique to AI initiatives.

- Assume you already understand conventional project management.

I have leveraged GenAI large language Models to research and refine these guidelines, ensuring rapid synthesis of cutting-edge insights, thorough coverage of critical AI-specific nuances, and the delivery of a clear, coherent framework for practitioners.

2.0 Defining Innovative AI Projects

Innovative AI projects are initiatives that introduce novel applications, techniques, or value propositions in AI — often challenging established norms in technology, business strategy, or societal outcomes. They differ from traditional IT projects due to:

- **Uncertain outcomes** (experimental nature of AI models).
- **Dependence on high-quality data**
- **Complex algorithms**
- **Ethical and regulatory complexities**.

In the swiftly evolving domain of artificial intelligence, not all projects are created equal—nor should they be approached with a one-size-fits-all mindset. The diversity of AI initiatives, ranging from evolutionary enhancements to paradigm-shifting innovations, necessitates a nuanced understanding of their nature and intent. Managing an AI project without recognizing its distinct characteristics can lead to misaligned rigor, misplaced expectations, and unintended consequences.

The below categorization offers a practical lens through which stakeholders such as developers, decision-makers, or policymakers can identify the type of AI project at hand and align governance, risk management, and resource allocation accordingly. By appreciating the purpose behind each initiative, we enable more responsible innovation, targeted oversight, and ultimately, outcomes that serve their intended goals with integrity and impact.

2.1 Types of AI Projects

1. **Incremental Innovation**

   Enhances existing end user AI systems through performance tuning, optimization, or feature expansion without fundamentally altering the core technology.
   - **User**: Business/customer end-users.
   - **Output**: Upgraded applications.

Example: Improving a recommendation engine by incorporating user sentiment analysis for better personalization; faster fraud detection SaaS product

2. **Disruptive Innovation**

*Introduces **novel end-user AI applications** that redefine markets or business models through radically new capabilities.*

- **User:** Customers/industries.
- **Output:** Transformative products.

Example: Deploying autonomous vehicles that replace human drivers and redefine transportation logistics; AI powered diagnostic tools.

3. **Applied Research Projects**

*Explores **novel algorithms or architectures** for advancing AI capabilities, with outputs feeding into end-user applications or AI enabler tools (see below).*

- **User:** Researchers → later integrated by developers.
- **Output:** Prototypes.

Example: Creating a new transformer variant optimized for real-time translation in low-bandwidth environments; Efficient LLM architectures.

4. **AI Enabler Projects**

Develops tools, platforms, or frameworks that empower the development, operation, and governance of other AI systems. This includes tools for building responsible, efficient, scalable AI, and platforms for creating advanced capabilities such as autonomous agents.

- **User:** AI engineers, developers, data scientists, ethics officers, and (in the case of democratization platforms) business professionals.
- **Output:** SDKs, APIs, platforms, agentic frameworks, orchestration tools.

Examples:

- Infrastructure & MLOps: MLOps pipelines (e.g., Kubeflow), data versioning tools (e.g., DVC).
- Responsible AI: Ethical compliance tools (e.g., bias detectors, explainability dashboards).
- Democratization: No-code/low-code AI builders (e.g., Teachable Machine).
- Frameworks for building and orchestrating AI agents (e.g., LangChain, AutoGen), platforms for developing tool-integrated autonomous systems.

5. **Citizen-led Innovation**

Empowers non-technical domain experts to create AI solutions from simple models to sophisticated automated agents that tackle specific challenges using no-code/low-code platforms and agent-building tools.

- **User**: Domain experts (e.g., business process owners, teachers, marketers, analysts).
- **Output**: Custom applications, automated content, and autonomous workflows and multi-step AI agents that automate complex tasks.

Examples:

- A teacher using Teachable Machine to build a custom AI model for sign language practice.
- A supply chain manager using an agent platform like Microsoft Copilot Studio to create an AI agent that monitors inventory, predicts shortages, and automatically generates and places purchase orders.
- A marketing professional automating a complex campaign workflow where an AI agent analyzes performance data, generates new content variants, and adjusts ad spending across platforms.

For an extended list of real-world projects mapped to the specified project type classifications please refer to Appendix A.

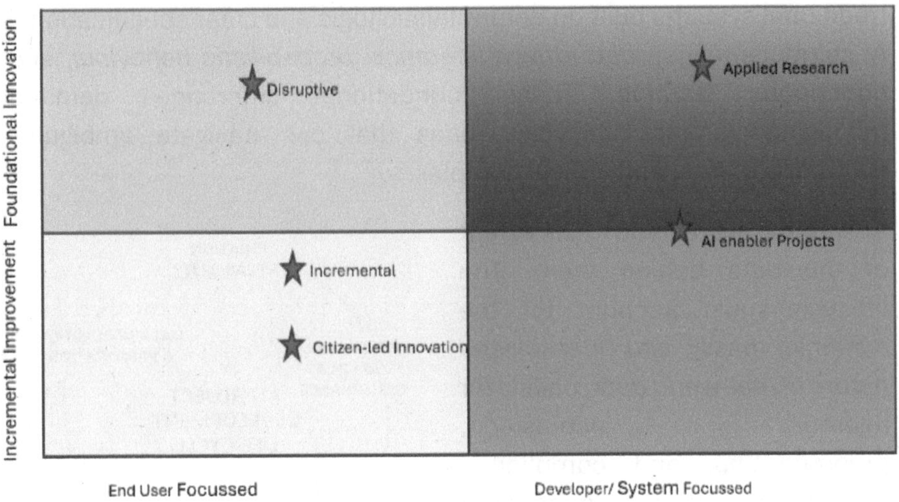

Figure 2.1 AI Project Typology Framework

3.0 AI Project Lifecycle (APLC)

Artificial Intelligence projects may resemble software development on the surface but beneath lies a fundamentally different beast. Unlike traditional systems built on deterministic logic and clear specifications, AI solutions rely on *data-driven inference, probabilistic behaviour,* and *continuous learning*. These foundational differences demand reimagined project lifecycles—ones that can navigate ambiguity, evolving patterns, and ethical complexity.

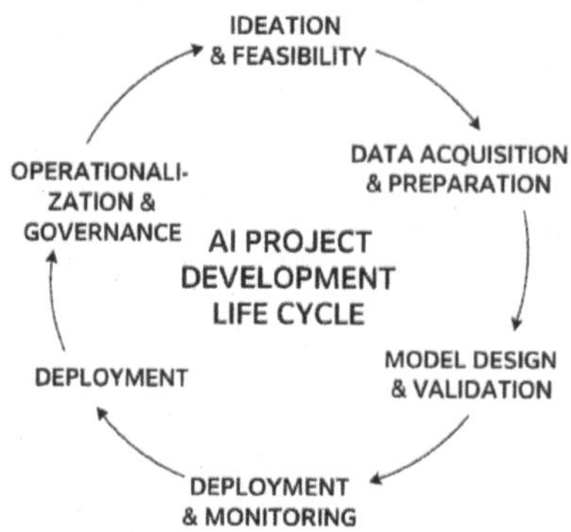

Figure 3.1 AI Project Life Cycle

AI systems are reliable to the extent of the data behind them. The lifecycle must account for the *dynamic, messy, and often biased nature of real-world data*, calling for rigorous acquisition, preprocessing, and compliance mechanisms—from annotation strategies to tools like data versioning and synthetic augmentation. Unlike conventional code, an AI model's behaviour is shaped less by fixed instructions and more by patterns learned, which makes *validating its reasoning and ensuring fairness* significantly more challenging.

Model performance is rarely static. AI models are susceptible to drift, requiring *continuous monitoring, recalibration, and transparency* throughout their operational life. Conventional deployment checklists fall short here; AI needs observability frameworks that not only track performance decay but also align with evolving social norms and regulatory expectations.

AI solutions must embed governance frameworks from the start—ensuring explainability, auditability, and fairness—especially in high-stakes domains. This lifecycle, therefore, integrates *ethics and oversight as first-class design principles*, not afterthoughts.

AI innovation thrives at the intersection of experimentation and structure. A hybrid approach—blending Agile adaptability with milestones for feasibility, data readiness, model validation, deployment, and governance—ensures that iterative progress aligns with purpose and risk.

What follows is a structured lifecycle tailored for AI development, integrating these dimensions. It recognizes not only the technical workflow, but also the evolving accountability that accompanies every stage.

3.1 Distinct phases of APLC

3.1.1 Phase 1: Ideation & Feasibility

This foundational phase sets the strategic and ethical intent for AI initiative. It aligns business objectives with stakeholder values, assesses technical viability, anticipates risks, and lays a responsible groundwork for all subsequent phases.

1. Strategic & Ethical Scoping

- Articulate clear business goals mapped to KPIs and user needs.
- Conduct stakeholder mapping to capture diverse perspectives and success criteria.
- Embed human-centred design principles to ensure AI solutions serve societal values and ethical norms.

2. Feasibility Assessment

- Data Availability & Quality: explore primary vs. secondary sources, assess sampling bias, and verify licensing constraints.
- Estimate computational Requirements: estimate compute, storage, and latency needs using prototype benchmarks.
- Regulatory & Organizational Fit: align with GDPR, sector regulations, and internal governance policies.

3. Hybrid Requirements Modelling & Estimating

- Apply hybrid modelling techniques to capture evolving requirements, merging user stories, data-driven insights, and prototype learnings.

- Evaluate COSMIC functional-sizing and effort-estimating approaches (www.cosmic-sizing.org) to quantify scope and estimate efforts.
- Define explicit ethical guardrails such as privacy, fairness, and transparency alongside functional specifications.
- Iterate in rapid sprints, continuously refining requirements as models and use cases co-evolve.

4. Premortem Analysis & Risk Stress-Testing

- Host premortem workshops to identify potential failure modes, root causes, and mitigation strategies.
- Create an early risk register covering technical, legal, operational, and ethical dimensions.
- Prioritize high-impact, high-likelihood risks for proof-of-concept focus.

5. Standards & Vocabulary Alignment

- ISO/IEC 22989:2022 for unified AI concepts and terminology.
- ISO/IEC 42001:2023 for establishing an AI management system (AIMS) framework.
- ISO/IEC 42005:2025 to guide early AI system impact assessments.
- ISO/IEC TR 24030:2024 to standardize and catalogue AI use cases.
- ISO/IEC 19761:2011 (Reviewed in 2025) for functional size measurement.

6. Emerging AI-Assisted Ideation Tools

- Leverage AI as a co-creator: adopt platforms that support divergent/convergent thinking and semantic clustering (Ye et al., 2025).
- Use prototyping environments with integrated ideation modules to blend AI suggestions with human creativity.
- Guard against automation bias by preserving human agency and maintaining critical evaluation loops.

3.1.2 Phase 2: Data Acquisition & Preparation

High-quality data underpins every successful AI initiative. This phase focuses on sourcing, cleansing, annotating, and governing datasets so they are accurate, unbiased, and ready for model development.

1. Data Sourcing & Licensing

- Inventory primary (in-house, sensors) and secondary (public, commercial) sources.
- Perform licensing and usage checks on open repositories to avoid IP or privacy violations.
- Incorporate marketplace benchmarks (Chen et al., 2023) to evaluate dataset completeness, cost, and format standardization.

2. Data Cleaning & Annotation

- Start with a representative subset to validate cleaning workflows (handling missing values, outliers, schema mismatches).
- Use semi-automated annotation tools and human-in-the-loop review to ensure label accuracy and consistency.
- Apply bias detection tests (e.g., disparate impact ratio) early to correct under-represented segments.

3. Versioning & Synthetic Data

- Employ data version control systems (DVC, Quilt) to track snapshots, transformations, and lineage.
- Generate synthetic samples for scarce or sensitive classes using GANs or rule-based simulators to bolster diversity.
- Maintain immutable storage of each data version to support auditability and rollback.

4. Data Readiness Assessment

Adopt Deloitte's AI Data Readiness (AIDR) framework across five dimensions: availability, quality, structure, security, and use-case alignment.

- Score each dimension on maturity scales to prioritize remediation efforts before modelling.
- Reassess readiness after major pipeline changes or source additions.

5. Governance & Metadata Management

- Define roles: data engineers ingest and transform; stewards enforce quality and lineage; scientists explore and validate.
- Use Guide to Data Management Body of Knowledge DAMA DMBOK v2 governance wheel to assign accountability for standards, metadata schemas, and master-data controls.
- Record data provenance in a centralized catalogue to facilitate audits and compliance checks.

6. Standards & Tooling Integration

- ISO/IEC 20546:2019 for unified big-data vocabulary and end-to-end pipeline stages (ingestion → storage → processing).
- ISO/IEC 8183:2023 to structure AI data life-cycle actions from acquisition through decommissioning.
- Control A.7 of ISO/IEC 42001:2023 – Artificial Intelligence Management System mandates documented processes for data management in AI systems.
- Align with Google's Rules for Machine Learning: build first pipelines in production-like environments, integrating training and monitoring.

7. Emerging Trends & Best Practices

- Embrace data-centric AI research: develop marketplace-style dataset benchmarks and transparent quality metrics (Chen et al., 2023).
- Leverage knowledge graphs to unify heterogeneous sources and enhance semantic interoperability (Jain et al., 2024).
- Automate anomaly detection on incoming data streams to flag quality drifts before modelling cycles.

3.1.3 Phase 3: Model Design & Validation

In this phase, algorithmic experimentation takes centre stage. Teams iterate on candidate architectures such as transformer networks and reinforcement-learning agents to gradient-boosted trees, while balancing predictive performance, fairness, explainability, and robustness.

1. Architecture Exploration

- Transformer and sequence-to-sequence models for NLP tasks.
- GenAI-specific architectures: Diffusion models for multimodal generation, retrieval-augmented generation (RAG) frameworks, and decoder-only LLMs.
- Agentic AI systems: Multi-agent orchestration (e.g., via AutoGen), planning modules, and tool-integrated agents (e.g., LangChain).
- Reinforcement-learning agents (e.g., via Hugging Face TRL library) for decision-making flows.
- Classical algorithms (random forests, gradient-boosted trees) for tabular data baselines.
- Nested-model approach (Dubey et al., 2024) layering validation checks from unit tests to system-level integrity gates.

2. Key Performance Dimensions

- Accuracy vs. Fairness: Trade-offs measured via demographic parity, equalized odds, and group-wise ROC curves.

- GenAI Quality: Perplexity, hallucination rates, coherence scores (e.g., BLEU, ROUGE), and output diversity.
- Agentic Efficacy: Task completion rate, goal alignment efficiency, and collaboration metrics in multi-agent systems.
- Robustness: Stress-testing against input perturbations, adversarial prompts, and environment shifts.
- Explainability: SHAP/LIME reports + GenAI-specific techniques (attention visualization, contrastive explanations).

3. Validation Techniques

- Cross-validation: k-fold, stratified, and time-series splits.
- A/B Testing: Canary rollouts and for GenAI/Agentic: Human preference scoring (e.g., RLHF) and conversation log analysis.
- Scenario-based Simulation: Digital-twin environments + Agentic extensions: Multi-agent conflict resolution sandboxes (Dahmen et al., 2023).
- GenAI Benchmarks: HELM, BIG-bench, and domain-specific prompt-injection resilience tests.
- Agentic Validation: Goal-tree verification and failure-mode testing for autonomous action sequences.

4. Experiment Tracking & Management

- MLflow Model Registry for artifact versioning and lineage.
- GenAI-specific tracking: Prompt versioning, response variation catalogues, and safety flag logs.
- TensorBoard for training visualization and for Agentic AI: Action trajectory mapping.
- Weights & Biases for collaborative dashboards with conversation replay and agent decision logs.

5. Hyperparameter Optimization

- Automated search; Temperature/top-p sampling sweeps and prompt compression ratio tuning
- Grid/random search + early stopping rules.
- Agentic considerations: Exploration-exploitation balance tuning for action policies.

6. Reproducibility & Scalability

- Containerization (Docker) + orchestration (Kubeflow, Airflow).
- GenAI/Agentic scaling: GPU memory optimization and distributed agent coordination backends.
- Embedded CI/CD gates for linting/testing/deployment.
- Infra-as-code (Terraform, Helm) + LLMOps patterns for prompt pipeline management.

7. Governance & Risk Management

- ISO/IEC AWI 23053 Modular ML framework
- ISO/IEC 5338 AI lifecycle processes
- ISO/IEC 23894 Risk mitigation
- ISO/IEC 42001:2023 AI governance.
- ISO/IEC 22989:2022 Terminology
- ISO/IEC 42005:2025 Impact assessments
- ISO/IEC 5259 Data-quality standards
- NIST GenAI Risk Framework (2024), Agentic System Audit Guidelines

8. Emerging Trends & Best Practices

- Continual-learning validation + GenAI real-time adaptation: Dynamic RAG index updating.

- Explainable-by-design: Built-in interpretability + GenAI transparency: Source attribution tagging.
- Ethics-first validation: Early fairness tests + Agentic safeguards: Value-alignment constraint embedding.
- Hybrid simulation: Real-world A/B tests + GenAI/Agentic digital twins:
    - **GenAI**: Human-in-the-loop red teaming environments.
    - **Agentic**: Multi-agent economic simulation arenas.

3.1.4 Phase 4: Deployment & Monitoring

Once AI models are validated, they are pushed into production via APIs, cloud endpoints, containers, or edge devices. This phase must balance operational stability with continuous oversight, embedding robust monitoring, alerting, and recalibration processes to catch drift, security threats, performance degradation, and for Agentic AI, logical failures, and state errors early.

1. Deployment Architecture & Governance

- Package models as Docker/Kubernetes services or serverless endpoints for consistency across environments. Deploy orchestration controllers, tool APIs, and state management databases for Agentic AI.
- Follow the ISO/IEC 23053 ML framework for system design, ensuring modularity, version control, and clear model–data separation.
- Apply PDCA governance per ISO/IEC 42001: define deployment policies (Plan), roll out via CI/CD (Do), monitor outcomes (Check), and refine processes (Act).

2. Mapping Drift Detection to NIST AI RMF Controls
Drift monitoring aligns with the AI RMF "Measure" and "Manage" functions.

- **MEA-1:** Continuously measure model performance and data characteristics (e.g., feature distributions, prediction accuracy). Measure conversation flow integrity and planning efficiency for Agentic AI systems.

- **MEA-2:** Track changes in operational metrics (latency, error rates) and data statistics (population shifts, schema changes). Consider tool invocation latency and success rates for Agentic AI.
- **MAN-1:** Automate alerts when metrics breach thresholds; document corrective actions (retraining, feature re-engineering, or agent logic patches).
- **MAN-2:** Implement governance workflows for model updates, ensuring traceability from drift detection through remediation.

3. Monitoring Toolkits & Real-Time Tracking

- Prometheus for system-level metrics (CPU, memory, latency).
- SageMaker Model Monitor or Evidently AI for model-specific metrics: data drift, target drift, prediction stability. For Agentic AI, extend monitoring to include:
    - **Conversation/Action Loops:** Track steps to task completion and detect infinite loops.
    - **Tool Invocation:** Monitor success/failure rates of API calls and external tool usage.
    - **State Persistence:** Ensure the agent's memory or context is maintained correctly across sessions.
- Evidently AI offers 100+ pre-built metrics and test suites, live dashboards, and integration with Grafana or BI tools for real-time observability.

4. Alerting, Thresholds & Automated Responses

- Define guardrails: e.g., trigger alerts if data drift > X %, accuracy drops below Y %, or, for Agentic AI, if tool failure rate exceeds Z % or a conversation exceeds a maximum step count.
- Use Prometheus Alertmanager or cloud alerts to notify teams.

- Automate pipelines: on drift alert, spin up a retraining job, validate new model, and swap endpoints only after quality gates pass.

5. Trustworthiness & Robustness per ISO Guidance

- Incorporate ISO/IEC 24028 to monitor bias and fairness metrics over time.
- Use ISO/IEC 24029-1 to assess neural-network robustness, running adversarial-test suites in production.
- Periodically review logs and audit trails to satisfy ISO/IEC 38507 governance requirements and maintain accountability.

6. Security & Resilience: Latest Best Practices

- Follow CISA's Joint Guidance on Deploying AI Systems Securely: enforce endpoint authentication, encrypt data in transit, and conduct vulnerability scans regularly.
- For Agentic AI, pay special attention to the security of all connected tools and APIs, as they represent a large attack surface.
- Segment networks and apply role-based access controls to AI resources.
- Maintain rolling backups of model artifacts, agent configurations, and state data to enable rapid rollback in case of compromise.

7. Advanced Observability Frameworks

- Adopt a multi-layered observability stack:
  - **Data layer:** capture feature distributions, schema changes.
  - **Trace layer:** distributed tracing of inference calls.
  - **Visualization layer:** real-time dashboards with sub-second refresh, historical trend analysis.

- Leverage AI-driven anomaly detection to reduce alert noise and improve mean time to resolution.

8. Operational Excellence with MLOps & GenAIOps

- Standardize CI/CD pipelines that include linting, static analysis, unit/integration tests, and production rollout steps.
- Maintain distinct sandboxes for development, testing, and production, ensuring governance policies are enforced uniformly.
- Establish an AI Center of Excellence to govern resource sharing, budgeting, and end-to-end lifecycle management.

3.1.5 Phase 5: Operationalization & Governance

Once models are deployed, operationalization and governance transform AI from isolated proofs-of-concept into sustainable, enterprise-wide capabilities. This phase ensures responsible scaling across teams and geographies by embedding lifecycle management, continuous learning, structured audits, version control, transparent update mechanisms, and human oversight.

1. Governance Framework & Accountability

Apply **ISO/IEC 38507** to establish board-level AI governance. Define roles for executive sponsors, data stewards, ethical reviewers, and cross-functional committees. Maintain audit trails of decisions, risk registers, and approval workflows to ensure traceability and alignment with strategic objectives.

2. Standardize Use Cases & Scaling

Leverage **ISO/IEC TR 24030** to catalogue AI Assets/ AI use cases across domains. Create a centralized repository of standardized templates to streamline requirements gathering, accelerate replication, and foster cross-team collaboration and knowledge sharing.

3. Lifecycle Management & Version Control

Implement robust lifecycle management using CI/CD pipelines and model registries. Tools like MLflow, Kubeflow, and GitHub Actions help version code, data, and model artifacts. As emphasized by Martyr (2025), managing the AI lifecycle—especially for LLM-based systems—requires collaborative infrastructure that supports experimentation, deployment, and optimization at scale.

4. Continuous Learning & Monitoring

Embed feedback loops and human-in-the-loop gates to capture user corrections and edge-case labels. Automate monitoring of performance, fairness, and data drift, triggering retraining pipelines when thresholds are breached. Tools such as Evidently AI provide built-in metrics dashboards and alerts for real-time observability.

5. Compliance & Auditing

Align governance processes with NIST AI RMF "Manage" controls and emerging regulations like the EU AI Act. Schedule periodic audits of model updates, decision logs, and access records. Document review findings and remedial actions in a centralized compliance log to support external reviews and certifications.

6. Human Oversight & Transparency

Produce model cards and datasheets that document each model's purpose, performance, training data, limitations, and fairness metrics. Implement human-review gates for high-stakes decisions and establish clear recourse mechanisms. Conduct regular training for stakeholders on ethical AI principles and governance standards to reinforce accountability.

7. Tools, Platforms & Best Practices

Implementing operationalization requires specialized tools for monitoring, governance, and workflow automation. For an overview of industry-standard solutions see Appendix B: Tooling for AI Operationalization. Establish an AI Center of Excellence (CoE) to maintain templates, share best practices, and audit adherence across distributed teams.

A summary of the above phases and key focus areas of each of the phases are tabulated in figure 3.2.

No.	Phase	Key Focus
1	Ideation & Feasibility	Define objectives, assess ethical and technical viability
2	Data Acquisition & Preparation	Source, clean, label data; ensure fairness and compliance
3	Model Design & Validation	Experiment with models, evaluate fairness and robustness
4	Deployment & Monitoring	Roll out, track drift, ensure user-facing transparency
5	Operationalization & Governance	Scale responsibly, implement audit and update frameworks

Figure 3.2 Life Cycle Phases and Key Focus Areas

4.0 Risk Management for success in AI Projects

Innovative AI projects hold immense potential to transform industries, enhance efficiency, and unlock new possibilities. However, their success is inherently tied to a proactive approach toward risk mitigation. Risks in AI projects can be broadly classified into four key categories: technical, operational, ethical & legal, and stakeholder risks. Each of these categories provides a structured framework for identifying challenges and developing effective mitigation strategies.

Technical risks encompass issues like model reliability, scalability, and security vulnerabilities, which can directly impact the performance and trustworthiness of AI systems. Operational risks involve implementation challenges, resource allocation, and adaptability within existing workflows. Ethical & legal risks address concerns related to bias, fairness, privacy, and compliance with evolving regulations to ensure responsible AI deployment. Stakeholder risks revolve around user acceptance, societal impact, and alignment with business objectives, as AI adoption relies on seamless collaboration across various interest groups.

4.1 Core Principles

Risk management for AI should be:

- **Integrated:** Align enterprise risk management with AI risks using ISO 31000:2018 and The National Institute of Science and Technology's Risk Management Framework (NIST AI RMF) Core functions (Identify, Protect, Detect, Respond, Recover).
- **Comprehensive:** Cover technical, security, ethical, legal, operational, and third-party risks.
- **Lifecycle-centric:** Embed checks at data ingestion, model training, validation, and runtime per ISO/IEC 23053 and Monetary Authority of Singapore's Model Risk Management practices (MAS MRM).
- **Adaptive:** Use red-teaming and adversarial testing frameworks such as Microsoft's Counterfit toolkit to uncover emerging threats.

- **Transparent:** Maintain explainability, audit trails, and stakeholder communication channels as recommended by Wharton AIRS.
- **Continuous:** Automate drift detection, bias monitoring, and performance tracking using SentinelOne's best practices to watch for bias and drift.

4.2 Establishing the Framework

Organizations must set up a governance structure that includes:

- Executive sponsorship with clear accountability
- Defined roles for data scientists, engineers, ethicists, and risk officers.
- Integration with existing IT and AI governance bodies as per ISO/IEC 38507 (governance implications of AI)
- Documented policies and procedures that tie risk appetite to AI objectives.

Figure 4.1 provides references for establishing components of the Risk Management Framework.

Component	Reference
Executive Oversight	Establish AI governance board per NIST AI RMF "Govern and Communicate" function.
Roles & Accountability	Define data stewards, model owners, security leads, and ethics officers following MAS MRM roles matrix.
Policies & Standards	Integrate ISO/IEC NP 38507 for IT governance implications of AI and Microsoft's AI security policies.
External Engagement	Participate in regulatory sandboxes and industry consortia (e.g., EU AI Act pilot projects).

Figure 4.1 Components of the Risk Management Framework

4.3 The Risk Management Process

The AI risk management process outlined below is structured into distinct but interconnected steps, each representing a critical phase in the systematic identification, assessment, mitigation, and oversight of risks across the AI lifecycle. These activities ensure that risks are managed proactively, transparently, and in alignment with both strategic objectives and compliance requirements.

4.3.1 Risk Identification

As AI systems become deeply embedded into core business functions, cultural institutions, and citizen services, managing their risks demands a multi-dimensional lens. These risks are not confined to algorithms or data—they span operational realities, ethical expectations, legal requirements, and stakeholder dynamics. This section categorizes AI-related risks into four major groups: **Technical**, **Operational**, **Ethical & Legal**, and **Stakeholder**. Each group addresses specific challenges that organizations must anticipate and navigate to ensure responsible, resilient, and trustworthy AI deployment.

Technical Risks - Data Quality & Availability, Model Performance & Scalability Challenges, Computational Resource Constraints, Robustness & Adversarial Attacks, Interpretability & Explainability Limitations, Integration & Compatibility Issues, Edge Cases & Generalization Failures.

Operational Risks - Infrastructure & Scalability, Data Management & Accessibility Issues, Talent & Skill Shortages, Integration Challenges with Legacy Systems, Operational Downtime & Resource Bottlenecks, Cost Management & Budget Constraints, Stakeholder Resistance & Change Management.

Ethical & Legal Risks – Bias & Discrimination in AI Models, Lack of Transparency & Explainability, Ethical AI Decision-Making & Accountability, Data Privacy & Consent Violations, Autonomy vs Human Control in AI Systems, Regulatory Compliance Challenges Liability Issues in AI-Driven Decisions, Intellectual Property & Copyright Concerns, Cybersecurity & AI System Vulnerabilities, Ethical AI Deployment in Sensitive Fields.

Stakeholder Risks - Misaligned Expectations Between Teams, Resistance to AI Adoption, Insufficient Stakeholder Engagement, Ethical Concerns from Customers & Regulators, Unrealistic ROI & Performance Expectations, Lack of AI Governance & Accountability, Poor Change Management & Transition Planning, Vendor & Third-Party Dependencies, Unrealistic Expectations from End-Users, Security & Data Breach Concerns from IT Teams.

NOTE: The same risk may appear across multiple categories (e.g., *Integration Challenges* under both Technical and Operational Risks, or *Explainability Limitations* under Technical and Ethical Risks). This is intentional, as risks are often multidimensional—their impact and mitigation strategies vary depending on the point of view (technical, operational, ethical, or stakeholder-centric). While this approach may introduce some redundancy, it ensures comprehensive coverage by addressing each risk within its relevant contexts.

4.3.2 Risk Assessment and Treatment

The AI risk assessment and treatment process is designed to provide a structured, evidence-based approach to identifying, analysing, and mitigating risks across technical, ethical, and operational dimensions. Building on the foundational steps outlined in ISO 31000:2018 and enriched by practical tools and guidance from the NIST AI Risk Management Framework (AI RMF), the following process supports proactive, context-sensitive risk management at scale. It helps

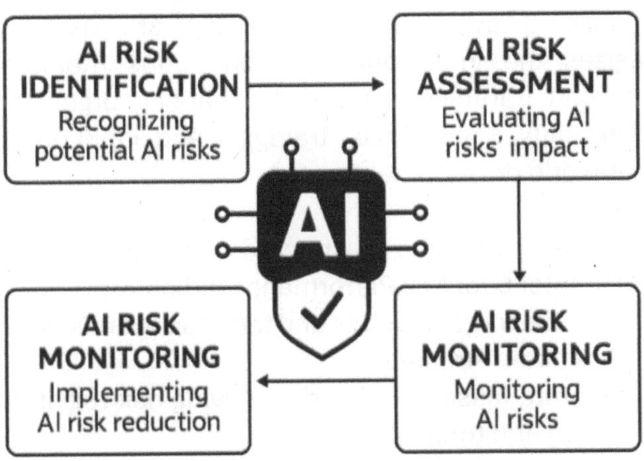

Figure 4.2 AI Risk Management

organizations transition from reactive compliance to forward-looking resilience and responsible AI governance.

1. **Identify:**
    - Map assets, data flows, and use cases.
    - Conduct workshops and scenario exercises (e.g., red teaming per Microsoft's framework).
2. **Analyse:**
    - Evaluate likelihood and impact using quantitative scoring.
3. **Evaluate & Prioritize:**
    - Use nested thresholds: evaluate at ERM, AI program, and individual model levels.
4. **Treat:**
    - Technical controls: adversarial training, data augmentation, model patching.
    - Organizational controls: approval gates, policy enforcement, legal reviews.
    - Deployment controls: canary releases, human-in-the-loop checks for high-risk outcomes.

A detailed taxonomy of risks and viable options for treatment is listed separately in Appendix C.

4.3.3 Monitoring, Review, and Improvement

To ensure AI systems remain trustworthy and responsive to evolving risks, ongoing oversight and learning are essential. This stage emphasizes the importance of continuous monitoring, structured reviews, and iterative refinement—enabling organizations to detect deviations early, improve risk strategies, and adapt policies in alignment with real-world developments.

- Embed real-time dashboards for key risk indicators (Refer Chapter 6 for Key Performance Indicators).
- Conduct regular audits and tabletop exercises using NIST AI RMF Playbook templates.
- Capture lessons learned in a living risk register, feed back into policy and training.

- Leverage academic insights on AI risk analytics to enhance predictive alerts.

4.3.4 Determining Human Oversight: The Probability-Severity-Harm Matrix

A critical output of the risk assessment phase is determining the appropriate level of human involvement required to mitigate identified risks. Not all AI decisions warrant the same level of oversight. A more strategic approach is to tailor human involvement based on the project's specific risk profile, using the Probability-Severity-Harm Matrix.

This framework, recognized in international standards like NIST's AI RMF and Singapore's Model AI Governance Framework, provides a pragmatic methodology for AI project leaders to make justified, consistent decisions about human-AI collaboration.

The matrix synthesizes two key dimensions from risk assessment:

- **Probability:** How likely is it that the AI system will cause harm or make a significant error?
- **Severity of Harm:** How serious would the impact be for stakeholders, the organization, or society if that error occurred?

By plotting these two factors, project managers can define a clear Human Oversight Strategy for different system outputs:

Probability/ Severity	**Low Severity**	**Medium Severity**	**High Severity**
Low Probability	Human-Out-of-The-Loop	Human-Over-The-Loop	Human-In-The-Loop (HITL)
	AI operates fully autonomously. Ideal for high-volume, low-risk tasks.	AI operates autonomously with human monitoring and the ability to intervene.	Human must review and approve every decision before action.
Medium Probability	Human-Over-The-Loop	Human-In-The-Loop (HITL)	Human-In-The-Loop (HITL)

Probability/ Severity	Low Severity	Medium Severity	High Severity
	AI operates autonomously with human monitoring and the ability to intervene.	Human must review and approve every decision before action.	Human must review and approve every decision before action.
High Probability	Human-In-The-Loop (HITL)	Human-In-The-Loop (HITL)	Human-In-The-Loop (HITL) mandatory
	Human must review and approve every decision before action.	Human must review and approve every decision before action.	If risk is unacceptable, reconsider the AI's role or the entire solution.

Figure 4.3 Probability – Severity – Harm Matrix

Integrating the Matrix into AI Project Management

For project leaders, this matrix is not merely an academic exercise but a vital tool for operational design and governance:

- **Informed Design Reviews:** During the Model Design & Validation phase (Section 3.1.3), use the matrix to mandate specific design requirements. A high-severity risk should trigger architectural choices that facilitate human review (e.g., explainability hooks, clear UI for decision support, API endpoints for approval workflows).
- **Resource Allocation and Budgeting:** The chosen level of oversight directly impacts operational costs. A requirement for "Human-in-the-Loop" for a high-volume process necessitates budgeting for human reviewers, their training, and the development of the oversight platform itself. This turns a risk mitigation strategy into a tangible line item in the project plan.
- **Stakeholder Alignment and Communication:** The matrix provides a clear, visual rationale for why human oversight is necessary (or not) for specific functions. This aligns technical teams, business leaders, and compliance officers on a shared

framework, moving the conversation from subjective debate to structured risk assessment.
- **Dynamic Governance:** The assigned level of oversight is not static. As model performance improves (lowering probability) or regulations change (affecting severity), the required level of human involvement should be re-evaluated during monitoring and review cycles (Section 4.3.3).

A Note on Implementation

Assigning probability and severity scores is a contextual exercise that requires input from domain experts, legal counsel, and ethical reviewers. The value of this framework lies in its ability to structure this critical discussion and ensure that decisions about human oversight are deliberate, documented, and proportional to risk, ultimately enabling teams to balance innovation with responsibility.

4.3.5 Key Process Steps Summary

Figure 4.4 provides summary of key activities of risk management process steps.

#	Step	Key Activities
1	Communication & Consultation	Engage stakeholders, share risk insights, capture diverse concerns
2	Scope, Context & Criteria	Define objectives, risk appetite, and internal/external factors
3	Risk Identification	Use threat modelling, red teaming, and scenario analysis to uncover vulnerabilities
4	Risk Analysis	Assess likelihood and impact across technical, ethical, and business dimensions
5	Risk Evaluation	Rank risks against tolerance thresholds to prioritize treatment
6	Risk Treatment	Apply controls: validation tests, bias mitigation, redundancy, human-in-the-loop reviews
7	Monitoring & Review	Track indicators, audit outcomes, update assessments
8	Recording & Reporting	Maintain logs of decisions, controls, and incident response

Figure 4.4 Risk Management Process Steps

4.4 ISO Standards as a reference

The International Organization for Standardization (ISO) offers a robust and evolving set of standards that address key risk domains in AI systems. These standards serve as foundational references to ensure clarity, consistency, and accountability across the AI lifecycle—from conceptualization and data handling to model design, deployment, and oversight. By embedding ISO guidelines into governance practices, organizations can align with global best practices, anticipate regulatory expectations, and strengthen the integrity and reliability of their AI solutions.

Domain	Standard Reference	Guidance
Terminology & Concepts	ISO/IEC 22989	Consistent Terminology
ML Lifecycle Framework	ISO/IEC 23053	Checkpoints at data prep, model validation
Bias & Fairness	ISO/IEC 24027	Statistical fairness tests, diverse data sourcing
Trustworthiness	ISO/IEC 24028	Explainability tools, ethics reviews
Robustness	ISO/IEC 24029-1	Adversarial testing, anomaly detection
Big Data Infrastructure	ISO/IEC 20546; 20547 series	Data governance, lineage tracking

Figure 4.5 ISO Guidelines for risk domains

AI risk management must extend to data ecosystems:

- Use ISO/IEC 20546 vocabulary to classify risks in data volume, velocity, and variety.
- Adopt the ISO/IEC 20547-1 for mitigating big data related vulnerabilities.
- Apply ISO/IEC 20547-3 architecture guidelines to design resilient, secure data pipelines.

4.5 AI Risks and Mitigations

This section provides a ready reference for major risks and recommendations for mitigations strategies.

Technical Risks:

#	Risk Name	Mitigation Strategy
1	Data Quality & Availability	Ensure high-quality datasets through preprocessing and bias correction.
2	Model Performance & Scalability	Use robust validation, continuous monitoring, and scalable architectures.
3	Computational Resource Constraints	Optimize algorithms, leverage efficient hardware, and cloud scalability.
4	Robustness & Adversarial Attacks	Employ adversarial training, robust model designs, and security measures.
5	Interpretability & Explainability	Utilize interpretable AI techniques such as SHAP values and LIME.
6	Integration & Compatibility Issues	Use standardized APIs, modular architectures, and thorough testing.
7	Edge Cases & Generalization Failures	Test extensively on edge cases and employ continuous learning techniques.

Figure 4.6a Technical Risks and Mitigations

Operational Risks:

#	Risk Name	Mitigation Strategy
1	Infrastructure & Scalability	Use cloud-based solutions, load balancing, and resource optimization.
2	Data Management & Accessibility	Establish strong data governance and standardize data pipelines.
3	Talent & Skill Shortages	Invest in training programs and leverage automation for efficiency.
4	Integration with Legacy Systems	Implement middleware and modular development approaches.
5	Operational Downtime & Bottlenecks	Develop monitoring systems, failover strategies, and redundancy plans.

#	Risk Name	Mitigation Strategy
6	Cost Management & Budget Constraints	Conduct ROI assessments, optimize cloud costs, and prioritize efficiency.
7	Stakeholder Resistance & Change Management	Provide AI literacy training and ensure transparency in implementation.

Figure 4.6b Operational Risks and Mitigations

Ethical Risks:

#	Risk Name	Mitigation Strategy
1	Bias & Discrimination	Conduct bias audits, diversify training data, and implement fairness-aware AI.
2	Transparency & Explainability	Use interpretable AI techniques and establish clear accountability.
3	AI Decision-Making & Accountability	Ensure human oversight and governance for high-risk AI applications.
4	Data Privacy & Consent	Implement privacy-enhancing techniques and strict access controls.
5	Autonomy vs Human Control	Define AI decision boundaries and reinforce human-in-the-loop processes.

Figure 4.6c Ethical Risks and Mitigations

Legal Risks:

#	Risk Name	Mitigation Strategy
1	Regulatory Compliance	Conduct legal reviews, maintain compliance frameworks, and stay updated on regulations.
2	Liability in AI Decisions	Define accountability measures and document AI decision processes clearly.
3	Intellectual Property Issues	Follow fair-use policies and ensure proper licensing for AI-generated content.
4	Cybersecurity & Vulnerabilities	Conduct security audits, adversarial training, and multi-layered authentication.
5	AI in Sensitive Fields	Follow industry-specific legal guidelines and establish ethical review boards.

Figure 4.6d Legal Risks and Mitigations

Stakeholder Risks:

#	Risk Name	Mitigation Strategy
1	Misaligned Expectations	Maintain clear communication and engage stakeholders in planning.
2	AI Adoption Resistance	Provide training programs and demonstrate AI's role in supporting humans.
3	Insufficient Engagement	Foster cross-functional collaboration and iterative feedback loops.
4	Ethical Concerns	Conduct ethics audits, ensure explainability, and maintain compliance.
5	Unrealistic ROI Expectations	Set realistic projections and provide phased implementation plans.
6	AI Governance & Accountability	Define roles, responsibilities, and ensure leadership oversight.
7	Change Management	Develop structured transition plans and secure stakeholder buy-in.
8	Vendor Dependencies	Establish contingency plans and negotiate strong vendor SLAs.
9	Unrealistic End-User Expectations	Educate users, document limitations, and maintain human oversight.
10	Security & Data Breach Concerns	Implement encryption, security audits, and AI risk assessments.

Figure 4.6e Stakeholders Risks and Mitigations

5.0 Tailoring AI Project Lifecycles

5.1 The Need for Tailored APLC

AI projects vary significantly in risk, complexity, and strategic impact. While the AI Project Life Cycle (APLC) provides a foundational framework, a one-size-fits-all approach fails to address critical variations in **scope, uncertainty, and ethical implications**. This chapter integrates two complementary frameworks to guide APLC customization:

1. **HBR's Risk/Impact Quadrants** (for project selection).
2. **Rigor-Based APLC Adaptation** (for execution).

5.2 Strategic Project Selection

In their 2024 publication *Mollick et al., Generative AI: The Insights You Need from Harvard Business Review (2024),* introduce a four quadrant framework for selecting GenAI projects. It also serves as a valuable lens through which APLC phases can be tailored to the type of AI solution being pursued ensuring alignment between project management intensity and the innovation it aims to deliver.

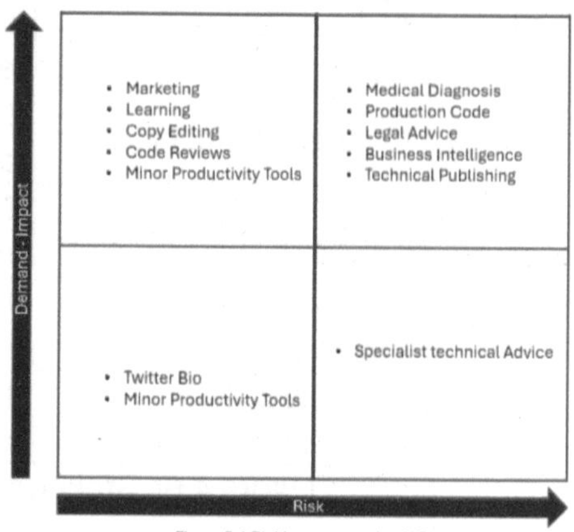

Figure 5.1 Picking a generative AI Project (adapted from HBR Project Selection Matrix)

Quadrant	Examples	Guidance
Low Risk/Low Impact	Twitter Bio, minor productivity tools	Experiment freely; minimal safeguards.
Low Risk/High Impact	Creative design, rapid prototyping	Scale aggressively; maximize ROI.
High Risk/Low Impact	Niche technical advice	Disproportionate risk.
High Risk/High Impact	Medical diagnosis, legal compliance	Deploy with extreme caution; require robust validation & oversight.

Prioritize *low-risk/high-impact* "sweet spots" for scalable innovation. Reserve *high-risk/high-impact* projects for transformative efforts with rigorous governance.

5.3 APLC Rigor Levels: Tailoring Execution to Project Needs

While the HBR quadrant framework provides a strategy for *selecting* Generative AI projects based on strategic intent and risk tolerance, real-world scenarios often present a different challenge: the necessity to *proceed* with projects regardless of their ideal placement on the matrix. Business imperatives, stakeholder expectations, or regulatory momentum may compel execution—even when uncertainty is high or readiness is incomplete.

In such cases, a suitably tailored AI Project Life Cycle (APLC) becomes critical. By introducing *appropriate levels of rigor,* the APLC compensates for potential gaps in feasibility, maturity, or clarity of purpose.

In this context, we introduce four levels of rigour as defined below for executing project life cycle phases.

Rigor Level	Key Traits	Ideal For
Low Rigor	Minimal processes Pre-built solutions Basic compliance	Citizen-led projects; no safety/legal risks.
Medium Rigor	Agile processes A/B testing Light governance	Incremental improvements; moderate risk.
High Rigor	Scientific/ethical scrutiny Reproducibility Bias audits	Applied research; ethics-driven projects.
Very High Rigor	Regulatory oversight Red-teaming Fail-safes	Disruptive innovation; life-critical AI.

5.4 Phase-Wise APLC Tailoring for Project Types

Align rigor levels with project characteristics across all APLC phases.

1. **Incremental Innovation**
    - **Rigor Level**: Medium
    - **Phase Adjustments**:
        - *Ideation*: Benchmark against existing solutions.
        - *Data Prep*: Augment data; automate feature engineering.
        - *Deployment*: Canary releases (not shadow-mode testing).
2. **Disruptive Innovation**
    - **Rigor Level**: Very High
    - **Phase Adjustments**:
        - *Ideation*: Prototype radically different approaches.
        - *Model Design*: Red teaming; novel architectures (e.g., hybrid RL+LLM).
        - *Deployment*: Shadow-mode testing; kill switches.
3. **Applied Research**
    - **Rigor Level**: High
    - **Phase Adjustments**:
        - *Ideation*: Literature reviews; SOTA benchmarks.
        - *Model Design*: Reproducibility tools (e.g., MLflow).
        - *Governance*: Third-party audits.
4. **AI Enabler Projects**
    - **Rigor Level:** High (Framework-dependent)
    - **Phase Adjustments:**
        - **Ethics & Governance**
            - **Data Prep:** Bias audits (e.g., IBM Fairness 360).
            - **Model Design:** Explainability-by-design (SHAP/LIME).
            - **Governance:** Mandatory third-party audits; compliance checks.
        - **Agentic AI Systems**
        - **Model Design:** Design for autonomous goal-seeking and tool-use; rigorous reward function shaping.

- **Testing:** Extensive simulation in sandboxed environments; adversarial testing for safety and alignment.
- **Deployment:** Hardened oversight mechanisms; real-time monitoring for unpredictable behavior; kill switches.

5. Citizen-Led Innovation

- **Rigor Level:** Low
- **Phase Adjustments:**
  - **Data Prep:** Leverage pre-built, curated datasets (e.g., Kaggle, Hugging Face).
  - **Model Design:** Use no-code/low-code platforms (e.g., Teachable Machine, Apple ML Create); explore simplified agentic workflows via platform-native tools.
  - **Deployment:** One-click deployment tools (e.g., Streamlit, Gradio).

5.5 Summary: Tailoring Alignment Chart

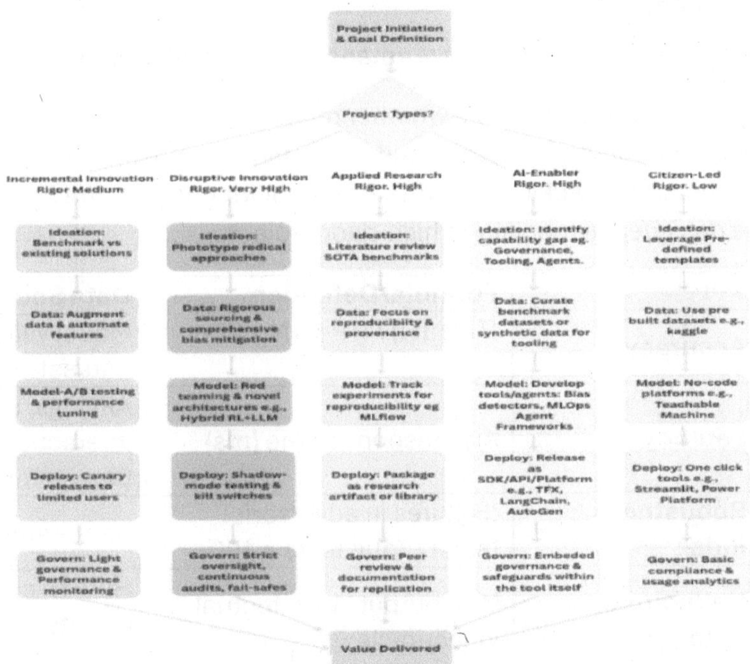

Fig 5.2 Tailoring APLC

6.0 Key Performance Indicators for AI Project Success

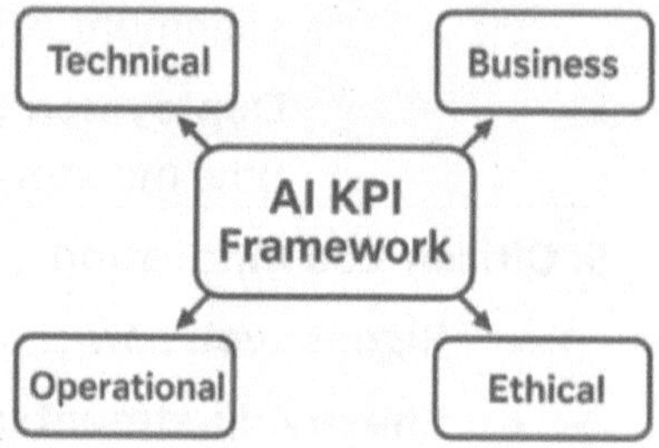

Figure 6.1 AI KPI Framework

In the dynamic landscape of innovative AI projects—spanning predictive ML, generative AI, and autonomous agentic systems—qualitative intuition alone cannot guarantee success. Quantifiable performance indicators are essential to objectively track progress, validate ROI, mitigate risks, and align technical execution with strategic goals. Without rigorous measurement, projects risk veering into inefficiency (e.g., uncontrolled cloud costs), ethical blind spots (e.g., undetected bias), or business misalignment (e.g., high-accuracy models with low user adoption). This chapter establishes a structured KPI framework categorized into **Technical, Business, Operational, and Ethical dimensions.**

6.1 Technical KPIs

Measure the functional performance and reliability of AI systems.

These indicators validate whether models meet technical specifications (e.g., accuracy, latency) and withstand real-world stressors (e.g., adversarial attacks, data drift). Essential for ensuring *the solution works as designed*, especially in high-rigor projects.

KPI	Formula/Definition	Data Source
Accuracy	(TP + TN) / (TP + TN + FP + FN)	Model validation datasets
Latency	Avg. response time (ms)	API logs, user interaction timestamps
Robustness Index	(Failures in adversarial tests) / Total tests × 100	Red-teaming logs
Hallucination Rate	% of outputs with factual inaccuracies	Human eval reports, fact-checking DB
Task Success Rate	(Completed user goals) / Total sessions	User session logs

KPI	Formula/Definition	Data Source
Context Adherence	% of outputs respecting provided context	LLM eval frameworks (e.g., LangSmith)

6.2 Business KPIs

Quantify strategic value and return on investment (ROI).

Track how AI solutions drive organizational goals—such as revenue growth, customer retention, or market differentiation. Aligns technical outputs with business outcomes to justify continued investment.

KPI	Formula/Definition	Data Source
ROI	(Net benefits - Project cost) / Project cost × 100	Finance systems
Customer Retention	% increase in repeat users	CRM analytics
NPS (AI Impact)	% Promoters - % Detractors	Post-interaction surveys
Time-to-Market	Days from ideation to production	Project management tools (Jira)
Adoption Rate	(Active users) / (Total eligible users)	Usage analytics (Mixpanel, etc.)
Cost per Inference	Total cloud cost / Inference volume	Cloud billing (AWS/GCP)

6.3 Operational KPIs

Monitor efficiency, scalability, and system health.

Focus on resource utilization (e.g., cloud costs), development velocity (e.g., deployment frequency), and operational stability (e.g., MTTD). Critical for balancing innovation with sustainable execution.

KPI	Formula/Definition	Data Source
Deployment Frequency	Number of releases/weeks	CI/CD pipelines (GitHub Actions)
Mean Time to Detect (MTTD)	Total downtime / Number of failures	Monitoring tools (Datadog, Prometheus)

KPI	Formula/Definition	Data Source
Training Time	Avg. hours per model iteration	ML experiment trackers (MLflow)
Cloud Cost Efficiency	(Planned spend - Actual spend) / Planned spend × 100	FinOps platforms (CloudHealth)
Model Drift Alert Rate	% of models triggering drift alerts	Drift detection tools (Evidently AI)
Resource Utilization	(GPU/Memory used) / Total allocated × 100	Kubernetes/kubectl

6.4 Ethical KPIs

Enforce Responsible AI practices and regulatory compliance.

Evaluate fairness, transparency, bias mitigation, and audit readiness. Non-negotiable for high-risk initiatives (e.g., healthcare, finance) to prevent harm and maintain trust.

KPI	Formula/Definition	Data Source
Fairness Score	1 - 'Δ between privileged/unprivileged groups'	Bias assessment tools (Aequitas)
Explainability Level	% of decisions with interpretable traces	XAI tools (SHAP, LIME)
Bias Threshold Compliance	% of features meeting fairness thresholds	Audit reports
Audit Pass Rate	(Passed audits) / Total audits × 100	Internal/third-party audit logs
User Consent Rate	% of users opting into data usage	Privacy management platforms (OneTrust)
Adversarial Robustness	% of attacks successfully defended	Security testing tools (Counterfit)

6.5 KPI Implementation Guide

1. **Data Collection Architecture**:
    - **Technical Metrics**: MLflow, Weights & Biases, LangChain logs

    - **Business Metrics**: Salesforce, Google Analytics, Finance ERP
    - **Operational Metrics**: Prometheus, CloudWatch, Datadog
    - **Ethical Metrics**: IBM Fairness 360, Aequitas, Audit trail DBs
2. **Calculation Frequency**:
    - Real-time: Latency, Resource Utilization
    - Daily: Adoption Rate, Cost per Inference
    - Weekly: Fairness Score, Deployment Frequency
    - Quarterly: ROI, Audit Pass Rate
3. **AI Type Customization**:
    - **GenAI**: Prioritize Hallucination Rate + Context Adherence
    - **Agentic AI**: Focus on Task Success Rate + Adversarial Robustness
    - **ML Projects**: Emphasize Accuracy + Model Drift Alerts

In managing AI innovation—from experimental GenAI to mission-critical agentic systems—the **categorized KPI framework (Technical, Business, Operational, Ethical)** transforms abstract goals into actionable intelligence. This structured measurement enables leaders to:

1. Diagnose real-time system health (e.g., hallucination rates, latency),
2. Validate strategic value (e.g., ROI, adoption),
3. Optimize resource leverage (e.g., cost per inference, deployment frequency), and
4. Enforce ethical guardrails (e.g., fairness scores, audit pass rates).

Critically, by scaling KPI monitoring intensity to match your project's rigor level (Chapter 4), organizations achieve *risk-proportional governance*:

- High-rigor projects (e.g., medical AI) demand real-time ethical/technical surveillance.

- Low-rigor initiatives (e.g., citizen-led tools) prioritize cost/agility metrics.

This dynamic approach turns KPIs from retrospective reports into proactive steering tools. Ensures every AI investment delivers measurable innovation while mitigating technical debt, ethical debt, and strategic misalignment.

7.0 Navigating the Future of AI Project Management

The guidelines presented here offer a structured yet adaptable approach to managing AI projects, ensuring they deliver value while mitigating risks. By applying this framework, organizations can:

- Identify project category based on project typology.
- Define Project Lifecycle using APLC framework.
- Recognize project's fit into HBR's quadrant model to balance risk and demand/ impact.
- Tailor project life cycle rigor (low to very high) to align with complexity and stake.
- Pre-empt failures through embedded risk mitigation across all phases of the AI Project Life Cycle (APLC).
- Measure success holistically with KPIs spanning technical, business, operational, and ethical dimensions.

Evolving with the AI Landscape

AI technology advances at a rapid pace, and so must tools and methodologies. While this guide references state-of-the-art tools, it is critical to:

- **Stay abreast of emerging technologies** and adopt newer, more efficient tools as they become available.
- **Continuously reassess workflows** to incorporate advancements in automation, interpretability, and governance.
- **Benchmark against industry standards** to ensure practices remain cutting-edge and compliant.

Critical Considerations for Sustainable AI

- **No Silver Bullet**: These guidelines are just a starting point, but the context matters. Adapt them to organization's regulatory environment, data maturity, and risk tolerance.
- **Dynamic Compliance**: AI regulations are evolving. Treat legal adherence as an ongoing process, not a one-time checkpoint.

- **Ethical Imperatives**: High-risk domains (e.g., healthcare, finance) demand proactive bias monitoring and transparency, even beyond legal requirements.
- **Human-Centric Design**: AI should augment human judgment, not replace it. Ensure solutions are explainable, accountable, and aligned with user needs.

AI's transformative potential is undeniable, but its success hinges on disciplined execution. Use these guidelines as a compass to:

- **Foster a culture of learning**, where teams iteratively improve processes and tools.
- **Prioritize collaboration** across technical, business, and ethical domains to bridge gaps in understanding.
- **Embrace agility** to pivot as technologies, regulations, and market demands shift.

The details related tools in this book including appendix are based on information shared by respective tool vendors and reviewers. The author has not independently verified the features or capabilities claimed by these sources. As with any evolving technology, readers are advised to exercise informed discretion and conduct due diligence before adopting or relying on any of the tools for critical applications.

Appendix A: Real-World Projects by Project Type

1. Incremental Innovation

Enhancing existing end-user AI applications.

1. **Netflix Recommendation Upgrades**
    - *Improvement*: Added temporal weighting for better fresh content suggestions.
    - *Reference*: Netflix Tech Blog
2. **Google Search BERT Integration**
    - *Improvement*: Better query understanding in 70+ languages.
    - *Reference*: Google AI Blog
3. **Amazon Alexa Context Carryover**
    - *Improvement*: Multi-turn conversation support.
    - *Reference*: Amazon Science
4. **Spotify Discover Weekly Enhancements**
    - *Improvement*: NLP-driven playlist personalization.
    - *Reference*: Spotify Engineering
5. **Tesla Autopilot Traffic Light Recognition**
    - *Improvement*: Added stoplight/stop sign detection.
    - *Reference*: Tesla Software Updates
6. **Grammarly Tone Detector**
    - *Improvement*: Real-time tone suggestions for writing.
    - *Reference*: Grammarly Engineering
7. **Adobe Photoshop Neural Filters**
    - *Improvement*: AI-powered skin smoothing and colorization.
    - *Reference*: Adobe Tech Blog
8. **Microsoft Excel Ideas Feature**
    - *Improvement*: Automated pattern detection in spreadsheets.
    - *Reference*: Microsoft Research
9. **Zoom Background Noise Suppression**
    - *Improvement*: Enhanced audio filtering using AI.
    - *Reference*: Zoom AI Research
10. **Uber ETA Accuracy Boosts**
    - *Improvement*: Real-time traffic prediction upgrades.
    - *Reference*: Uber Engineering

2. Disruptive Innovation

Novel end-user applications reshaping markets.

1. **Waymo Autonomous Taxis**
   - *Capability*: Driverless ride-hailing in Phoenix/SF.
   - *Reference*: Waymo
2. **OpenAI ChatGPT**
   - *Capability*: Human-like conversational AI.
   - *Reference*: OpenAI
3. **DeepMind AlphaFold**
   - *Capability*: Protein structure prediction (biology revolution).
   - *Reference*: DeepMind
4. **Boston Dynamics Atlas Robot**
   - *Capability*: Parkour-performing humanoid robot.
   - *Reference*: Boston Dynamics
5. **Stability AI Stable Diffusion**
   - *Capability*: Open-source text-to-image generation.
   - *Reference*: Stability.AI
6. **Notion AI Q&A**
   - *Capability*: Semantic search across documents.
   - *Reference*: Notion AI
7. **Midjourney v5**
   - *Capability*: Photorealistic image generation.
   - *Reference*: Midjourney
8. **Hugging Face HuggingChat**
   - *Capability*: Open-source alternative to ChatGPT.
   - *Reference*: Hugging Face
9. **Runway ML Gen-2**
   - *Capability*: Text-to-video synthesis.
   - *Reference*: Runway
10. **Anthropic Constitutional AI**
    - *Capability*: Self-correcting AI alignment.
    - *Reference*: Anthropic

3. Applied Research

Novel algorithms with real-world applicability.

1. **Meta AI Segment Anything Model**
   - *Breakthrough*: Zero-shot image segmentation.

- *Reference*: Meta AI Research

2. **Google Pathways Language Model**
   - *Breakthrough*: Multitask few-shot learning.
   - *Reference*: Google Research
3. **NVIDIA GauGAN3**
   - *Breakthrough*: Interactive photorealistic rendering.
   - *Reference*: NVIDIA Research
4. **DeepMind AlphaCode**
   - *Breakthrough*: Competitive programming AI.
   - *Reference*: DeepMind
5. **OpenAI Whisper**
   - *Breakthrough*: Robust multilingual speech recognition.
   - *Reference*: OpenAI
6. **Microsoft Turing-NLG**
   - *Breakthrough*: 530B-parameter language model.
   - *Reference*: Microsoft Research
7. **IBM Project Debater**
   - *Breakthrough*: AI for formal debate.
   - *Reference*: IBM Research
8. **Tesla Dojo Supercomputer**
   - *Breakthrough*: Custom AI training infrastructure.
   - *Reference*: Tesla AI Day
9. **Hugging Face BLOOM**
   - *Breakthrough*: Open multilingual LLM.
   - *Reference*: Hugging Face
10. **Anthropic Claude 2**
    - *Breakthrough*: Constitutional AI for harm reduction.
    - *Reference*: Anthropic

4. AI Enablers

Tools for developers/teams to build/govern AI.

1. **LangChain**
   - **Function:** Creating context-aware reasoning applications and multi-step AI agents that can use tools.
   - **Reference:** LangChain Official Website

2. **AutoGen**
    - **Function:** Enables LLM development of applications with multiple agents that can converse with each other to solve tasks.
    - **Reference:** AutoGen on GitHub
3. **IBM AI Fairness 360**
    - *Function*: Bias detection toolkit.
    - *Reference*: IBM Research
4. **Hugging Face Transformers**
    - *Function*: Pre-trained NLP model library.
    - *Reference*: Hugging Face
5. **Weights & Biases**
    - *Function*: Model performance visualization.
    - *Reference*: W&B
6. **Fairlearn**
    - *Function*: Fairness assessment for classifiers.
    - *Reference*: Microsoft
7. **Seldon Core**
    - *Function*: Kubernetes-native model deployment.
    - *Reference*: Seldon
8. **Evidently AI**
    - *Function*: Data drift monitoring.
    - *Reference*: Evidently AI
9. **Great Expectations**
    - *Function*: Data validation framework.
    - *Reference*: Great Expectations
10. **TensorFlow Privacy**
    - *Function*: Differential privacy for ML.
    - *Reference*: TensorFlow

5. Citizen-Led Innovation

Non-technical/ domain expert users solving problems with no-code AI.

1. **Microsoft Copilot Studio**
    - **Use Case:** Allows business users to build custom AI-powered copilots and conversational agents that can automate workflows, answer questions, and perform actions across business data and applications.
    - **Reference:** Microsoft Copilot Studio

2. **Airtable AI**
    - **Use Case:** Allows teams to build custom AI agents that summarizes tickets and suggests responses or a marketing agent that classifies leads and generates outreach copy—all through a no-code interface.
    - **Reference:** Airtable AI
3. **Google Teachable Machine**
    - *Use Case*: Teachers building custom image classifiers.
    - *Reference*: Google Creative Lab
4. **Microsoft Power Platform + AI Builder**
    - *Use Case*: Small businesses automating invoice processing.
    - *Reference*: Microsoft
5. **Runway ML Video Editing**
    - *Use Case*: Designers creating AI-generated backgrounds.
    - *Reference*: Runway ML
6. **Lobe by Microsoft**
    - *Use Case*: Farmers building crop disease detectors.
    - *Reference*: Lobe
7. **Zapier + OpenAI API**
    - *Use Case*: Marketers automating content generation.
    - *Reference*: Zapier
8. **Apple Create ML**
    - *Use Case*: Doctors training custom diagnostic models.
    - *Reference*: Apple Developer
9. **DataRobot AutoML**
    - *Use Case*: Nonprofits predicting donation patterns.
    - *Reference*: DataRobot
10. **NVIDIA Canvas**
    - *Use Case*: Artists converting sketches to landscapes.
    - *Reference*: NVIDIA

Appendix B: AI Operationalization Tooling Framework

Supporting Sections 3.1.5 (Operationalization & Governance), 4.0 (Risk Management), and 6.3 (Operational KPIs)

1. The Need for Specialized AI Tooling

This appendix offers a concise survey of the AI-powered tools that can augment how you research, create, analyse, and automate tasks. It explains why having a structured toolkit is essential in today's fast-moving digital landscape and defines the scope of what you will find here—ranging from natural language processors and computer-vision APIs to workflow-automation platforms.

AI systems introduce unique operational challenges that traditional software tools cannot address.

Core Challenges Requiring Dedicated Tools:

Challenge	AI-Specific Needs	Tooling Impact Areas
Reproducibility	Model/data version drift	Experiment tracking, artifact storage
Dynamic Performance	Concept/data drift in production	Real-time monitoring, alerting
Compliance Burden	Regulatory requirements	Audit trails, policy enforcement
Ethical Scalability	Undetected bias amplification at scale	Bias monitoring, fairness controls
Resource Volatility	GPU/compute spikes during inference	Auto-scaling, cost optimization

2. Categories of Tools

2.1 MLOps & Development Lifecycle Tools

Ensure reproducibility and collaboration across APLC phases.

Tool Type	Key Capabilities	Representative Solutions	Phase Alignment
Unified Workspaces	- Collaborative environments - Compute/resource management - Integrated version control	Domino Data Lab, Dataiku, Vertex AI	Phase 2-3 (Data/Model Dev)
Experiment Trackers	- Parameter/metric logging - Artifact storage - Visual comparisons	MLflow, Weights & Biases, Neptune	Phase 3 (Model Validation)
Pipeline Orchestration	- CI/CD automation - Dependency management - Error handling workflows	Apache Airflow, Prefect, Kubeflow Pipelines	Phase 4 (Deployment)

2.2 Production Monitoring & Observability

Maintain model health and performance in live environments.

Capability	Critical Metrics Tracked	Tool Examples	KPI Linkage (Section 6.3)
Performance Drift	- Accuracy decay - Latency/throughp	Fiddler, Aporia, Arize	Model accuracy, System latency

Capability	Critical Metrics Tracked	Tool Examples	KPI Linkage (Section 6.3)
	ut - Error rate spikes		
Data Drift	- Feature distribution shifts - Covariate drift - Outlier detection	Evidently, WhyLabs, Amazon SageMaker Monitor	Data quality index
Explainability	- Prediction reasoning - Feature attribution - Counterfactual analysis	SHAP, LIME, Fiddler Explainability	Interpretability score

2.3 Governance, Risk & Compliance (GRC)

Operationalize ethical and legal requirements.

Requirement	Tool Implementation	Specialized Solutions	Risk Linkage (Section 4.5)
Audit Trails	- Immutable decision logs - Model lineage tracking - Access records	IBM Watson Governance, Seldon Alibi	Legal/Compliance Risks (4.5.4)
Policy Enforcement	- Automated compliance checks - Regulation templates	Credo AI, Fairlearn, AuditAI	Ethical Risks (4.5.3)

Requirement	Tool Implementation	Specialized Solutions	Risk Linkage (Section 4.5)
	(GDPR/HIPAA) - Permission controls		
Bias Monitoring	- Disparate impact analysis - Fairness threshold alerts - Mitigation suggestions	Aequitas, Credo AI, TensorFlow Fairness	Stakeholder Risks (4.5.5)

3. Implementation Framework

3.1 Tool Selection Matrix

Match solutions to project characteristics (refer to Section 5.4 for tailoring to project types)

Project Profile	Priority Tool Categories	Recommended Stack
High-Risk (Healthcare/Finance)	1. GRC 2. Monitoring 3. Audit	IBM Watson Gov + Fiddler + Credo AI
Rapid Prototyping	1. MLOps 2. Lightweight Monitoring	MLflow + Evidently + Prefect
Enterprise Scale	1. Unified Workspace	Domino Data Lab + Airflow + Fiddler

Project Profile	Priority Tool Categories	Recommended Stack
	2. Orchestration	
Edge Deployment	1. Lightweight Monitoring 2. GRC Lite	BentoML + Evidently (Edge) + Credo AI Lite

3.2 Integration Roadmap

1. **Phase 3 (Model Design):** Embed governance scanners (Credo AI) and experiment trackers (MLflow)
2. **Phase 4 (Deployment):** Connect monitoring (Fiddler) and orchestration (Airflow)
3. **Phase 5 (Operationalization):** Activate GRC (IBM Watson) with automated audits.

Implement "Golden Path" pipelines - pre-configured toolchains for:

- Regulatory projects: IBM Watson → Fiddler → Credo AI
- Research projects: MLflow → Evidently → Prefect*

4. Tool Decision Flowchart

Select suitable category of tools based on project risk level and experience of the team members:

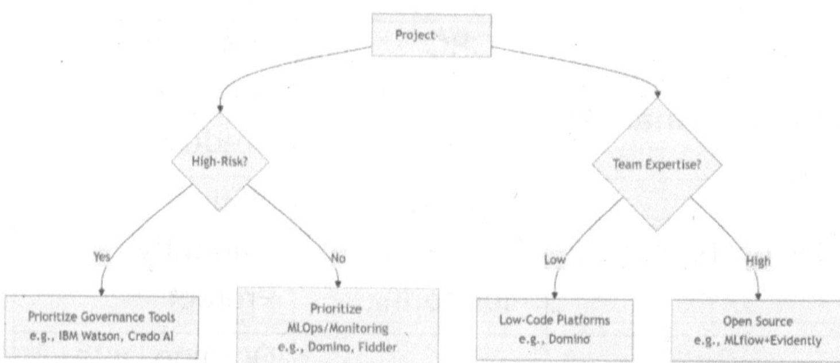

Figure B.1 Project Risk/ Team based Tool Selection

5. Vendor Comparison Guide

Solution	Strengths	Ideal For	Integration Complexity
IBM Watson Governance	End-to-end compliance workflows	Regulated industries	High (enterprise)
Domino Data Lab	Unified compute/resource management	Research-heavy teams	Medium
Credo AI	Ethical risk quantification frameworks	ESG-focused organizations	Low-Medium
Fiddler	Customizable monitoring dashboards	Production-critical systems	Medium

6. Cost-Benefit Analysis Framework

Evaluate tools using 4 dimensions (scale 1-5):

1. **Risk Coverage:** Compliance needs addressed
2. **Time Savings:** Reduction in manual processes
3. **Skill Fit:** Learning curve alignment
4. **TCO Reduction:** Cost vs. build-in-house

The AI tool ecosystem is evolving at breakneck speed, with innovative solutions appearing almost daily. While this appendix captures a snapshot of the most relevant offerings at the time of writing, it cannot—and does not—replace ongoing exploration. Readers are encouraged to actively monitor emerging solutions, experiment with new entrants, and periodically reassess their toolset to stay aligned with evolving technologies and context-specific needs.

Appendix C: Risk Taxonomy

Technical Risks

1. Data Quality & Availability Risks : AI models rely heavily on data, but insufficient, biased, or poor-quality datasets can lead to inaccurate predictions.
   Mitigation: Ensure high-quality, well-curated datasets through rigorous preprocessing, augmentation, and bias correction techniques.

2. Model Performance & Scalability Challenges : An AI model that performs well in lab conditions may fail when deployed at scale due to unseen scenarios.
   Mitigation: Use robust validation techniques, continuous performance monitoring, and scalable architectures to adapt to real-world conditions.

3. Computational Resource Constraints: AI models, especially deep learning models, require significant compute power, storage, and memory, which can be a bottleneck.
   Mitigation: Optimize algorithms, leverage efficient hardware (e.g., GPUs, TPUs), and utilize cloud-based resources for scalability.

4. Robustness & Adversarial Attacks : AI models can be vulnerable to adversarial manipulation, where slight perturbations in input data cause incorrect outputs.
   Mitigation: Employ adversarial training, robust model architectures, and security measures to counter potential vulnerabilities.

5. Interpretability & Explainability Limitations : AI models function as "black boxes," making it difficult to understand basis of their reasoning.
   Mitigation: Utilize interpretable AI techniques such as SHAP values, LIME explanations, and model-specific transparency methods.

6. Integration & Compatibility Issues : AI solutions often need to integrate with existing enterprise systems, which can lead to compatibility challenges.
   Mitigation: Use standardized APIs, modular development approaches, and conduct thorough integration testing.

7. Edge Cases & Generalization Failures: AI models may struggle with rare or unpredictable scenarios that were not represented in the training data.
   Mitigation: Perform extensive testing on edge cases, employ continuous learning techniques, and retrain models with diverse datasets.

Operational Risks

1. Infrastructure & Scalability Risks : AI systems require robust infrastructure, and inadequate computing power or network reliability can lead to inefficiencies and failures.
   Mitigation: Utilize cloud-based architectures for elasticity, ensuring scalable storage and computing power. Deploy load-balancing techniques and optimize resource allocation.

2. Data Management & Accessibility Issues: Poor data availability, fragmented data sources, and inconsistent formats can hinder AI performance.
   Mitigation: Establish strong data governance policies, create standardized data pipelines, and ensure seamless access across departments.

3. Talent & Skill Shortages : AI projects require specialized expertise, and a lack of skilled personnel can slow progress.
   Mitigation: Invest in continuous upskilling programs, partner with AI training providers, and leverage automation to reduce dependence on highly specialized talent.

4. Integration Challenges with Legacy Systems: AI tools often need to integrate with outdated enterprise systems, leading to compatibility issues.

Mitigation: Use modular development approaches, implement middleware solutions, and conduct extensive integration testing.

5. Operational Downtime & Resource Bottlenecks: Unexpected failures in AI models or dependencies can lead to service disruptions.
   Mitigation: Develop automated monitoring systems, implement failover strategies, and ensure redundancy in critical operational components.

6. Cost Management & Budget Constraints : AI projects can become expensive due to hardware costs, cloud usage, and ongoing optimization.
   Mitigation: Conduct thorough ROI assessments, optimize cloud resource consumption, and prioritize cost-effective AI solutions.

7. Stakeholder Resistance & Change Management : Resistance to adoption of AI by employees and/or decision-makers due to a lack of understanding or fear of job displacement.
   Mitigation: Ensure transparent communication, provide training programs, and implement AI in a way that complements human roles rather than replaces them.

Ethical Risks

1. Bias & Discrimination in AI Models : AI systems can inadvertently reinforce biases present in training data, leading to unfair outcomes in hiring, lending, healthcare, etc.
   Mitigation: Conduct bias audits, use diverse training data, and implement fairness-aware algorithms to minimize unintended discrimination.

2. Lack of Transparency & Explainability : AI models, especially deep learning are "black boxes," making it difficult to explain their decisions.
   Mitigation: Use interpretable AI techniques like SHAP values, LIME, and decision trees to improve model transparency and accountability.

3. Ethical AI Decision-Making & Accountability : AI systems making decisions without proper human oversight can lead to ethically questionable outcomes, such as biased automation in financial approvals.
   Mitigation: Ensure human-in-the-loop mechanisms, establish AI governance frameworks, and require justification for high-risk decisions.

4. Data Privacy & Consent Violations : AI models often process personal data, raising concerns about unauthorized use, data breaches, and privacy violations.
   Mitigation: Implement privacy-enhancing techniques like federated learning, differential privacy, and strict access controls.

5. Autonomy vs Human Control in AI Systems : Excessive automation can reduce human oversight, leading to errors in decision-making and unintended consequences.
   Mitigation: Define boundaries for AI autonomy, enforce human-in-the-loop mechanisms, and establish clear intervention protocols.

Legal Risks

1. Regulatory Compliance Challenges : AI projects must comply with laws such as GDPR (Europe), CCPA (California), and India's Digital Personal Data Protection Act.
   Mitigation: Conduct regular legal reviews, hire compliance officers, and maintain up-to-date knowledge of AI regulations.

2. Liability Issues in AI-Driven Decisions: If an AI system makes harmful or incorrect decisions (e.g., medical misdiagnosis or fraudulent transactions), liability becomes a concern.
   Mitigation: Define accountability measures, clearly document AI decision processes, and implement fallback mechanisms to mitigate harm.

3. Intellectual Property & Copyright Concerns : AI-generated content (e.g., artwork, code, text) raises questions about ownership and infringement on existing copyrights.
   Mitigation: Ensure proper licensing, follow fair-use policies, and attribute sources appropriately to avoid legal disputes.

4. Cybersecurity & AI System Vulnerabilities : AI models can be targets of hacking or adversarial attacks, compromising data integrity or causing malicious AI behaviour.
   Mitigation: Conduct security audits, use adversarial training to fortify models, and implement multi-layered authentication for AI-driven systems.

5. Ethical AI Deployment in Sensitive Fields: AI in areas like healthcare, law enforcement, and finance must adhere to strict ethical and legal standards to prevent harm.
   Mitigation: Follow industry-specific legal guidelines, establish ethical AI review boards, and ensure clear accountability structures.

Stakeholder Risks

1. Misaligned Expectations Between Teams : Different stakeholders—business leaders, developers, and users—may have conflicting expectations regarding AI capabilities, performance, or business impact.
   Mitigation: Establish clear communication channels, define realistic AI expectations, and involve key stakeholders in the planning and validation processes.

2. Resistance to AI Adoption : Employees may fear job displacement or struggle to trust AI recommendations.
   Mitigation: Provide AI literacy training, demonstrate how AI complements human roles, and ensure transparency in AI decision-making.

3. Insufficient Stakeholder Engagement : Lack of collaboration between domain experts and AI developers can lead to misinterpretation of business needs.

Mitigation: Foster cross-functional collaboration through workshops, involve stakeholders in user testing, and create iterative feedback loops.

4. Ethical Concerns from Customers & Regulators : Users and regulatory bodies may raise concerns about data privacy, bias, and AI fairness.
   Mitigation: Conduct regular ethics audits, implement explainable AI techniques, and ensure compliance with regulatory standards.

5. Unrealistic ROI & Performance Expectations : Business leaders might expect immediate returns without considering model training, deployment challenges, or maintenance costs.
   Mitigation: Set realistic ROI projections, provide phased implementation plans, and continuously measure AI performance against predefined benchmarks.

6. Lack of AI Governance & Accountability : Unclear ownership and accountability within an organization can led to confusion in AI project management.
   Mitigation: Define AI governance structures, assign roles and responsibilities, and ensure leadership oversight for AI initiatives.

7. Poor Change Management & Transition Planning : Implementing AI into existing workflows may disrupt established processes, leading to operational inefficiencies.
   Mitigation: Develop detailed AI transition plans, conduct pilot programs before full implementation, and ensure stakeholder buy-in for changes.

8. Vendor & Third-Party Dependencies : Relying on external AI models, cloud services, or data providers introduces risks related to service disruptions or lack of control over AI models.
   Mitigation: Establish contingency plans, negotiate strong SLAs with vendors, and maintain alternative AI solutions when possible.

9. Unrealistic Expectations from End-Users : End-users may expect AI systems to be infallible and autonomous beyond their current capabilities.
   Mitigation: Educate users on AI limitations, manage expectations through proper documentation, and ensure human oversight in critical AI decisions.

10. Security & Data Breach Concerns from IT Teams : IT and cybersecurity teams may worry about AI vulnerabilities, data security breaches, or adversarial threats.
    Mitigation: Implement robust security measures, encrypt sensitive data, and conduct regular AI security assessments.

References

Standards & Technical Documents

- **ISO/IEC 5259 series** — Data quality for analytics and machine learning
- **ISO/IEC 5338:2023** — Artificial intelligence — AI system life cycle processes
- **ISO/IEC 8183:2023** — Artificial intelligence — Data life cycle framework
- **ISO/IEC 19671:2011** — Functional size measurement (Reviewed in 2025)
- **ISO 31000:2018** — Risk management — Guidelines
- **ISO/IEC 20546:2019** — Big data — Overview and vocabulary
- **ISO/IEC 22989:2022** — Artificial intelligence — Concepts and terminology
- **ISO/IEC 23053:2022** — Framework for AI systems using machine learning
- **ISO/IEC 23894:2023** — Artificial intelligence — Guidance on risk management
- **ISO/IEC TR 24030:2024** — Artificial intelligence — Use cases
- **ISO/IEC 38507:2022** — Governance implications of artificial intelligence
- **ISO/IEC 42001:2023** — Artificial intelligence — Management system (AIMS) framework
- **ISO/IEC 42005:2025** — Artificial intelligence — Guidance for early AI system impact assessments
- **NIST (2023)** — AI Risk Management Framework

Articles & Reports

- **Chen, L., et al. (2023).** *Data acquisition: A new frontier in data-centric AI.*
- **Dahmen, U., Osterloh, T., & Roßmann, J. (2023).** *Structured validation of AI-based systems by virtual testing.*
- **Dubey, A., Yang, Z., & Hattab, G. (2024).** *A nested model for AI design and validation.*
- **Jain, N. S. (2024).** *Data preparation algorithm for AI workflows.*
- **McKinsey Global Institute. (2023).** *The state of AI.*
- **Mendez, F. (2020).** *Hybrid modeling for requirements in AI projects.*
- **Mollick, E., De Cremer, D., Neeley, T., & Sinha, P. (2024).** *Generative AI: The insights you need from Harvard Business Review.*
- **Plätke, O., & Geibel, R. C. (2024).** *The use of artificial intelligence for idea generation in the innovation process.*
- **Vazquez, D., et al. (2025).** *Preparing good data for generative AI: Challenges and approaches.*
- **Ye, R., et al. (2025).** *The design space of recent AI-assisted research tools for ideation, sensemaking, and scientific creativity.*

Industry & Organizational Resources

- **DAMA International. (2017).** *Data Management Body of Knowledge (DMBOK v2)*
- **Select Star. (2024).** *Data preparation for AI: Best practices and step-by-step guide*
- **Deloitte. (2023).** *Transforming AI outcomes with effective data readiness*

- **Futurium. (2024).** *Implementing AI governance: From framework to practice*
- **AI Standards Hub. (2023).** *Information technology — AI verification & validation*
- **Microsoft. (2024).** *Manage AI operations and deployment (MLOps & GenAIOps)*
- **Martyr, R. (2025).** *Managing the AI lifecycle in 2025: A comprehensive guide*
- **Quanta Intelligence. (2024).** *New standards for model validation in tech*
- **Evidently AI. (2024).** *Open-source ML monitoring and observability*
- **Google. (2023).** *Rules for machine learning*
- **Singapore PDPC. (n.d.).** *Singapore Model AI Governance Framework*
- **iTech Creations. (2023).** *Understanding data acquisition and data preparation for AI project cycle*
- **IBM. (2024).** *What is AI model lifecycle management?*

Endorsements

"Managing Innovative AI Projects" by Dr. Jayakumar K R and Prof. Alain Abran is an indispensable guide that bridges traditional project management and the unique demands of AI innovation. It equips project managers to adapt quickly with a robust, process-driven approach integrating an AI development lifecycle into organizational workflows. What makes it stand out is its focus on critical touchpoints, decision gates, and governance models essential to AI—offering practical frameworks that address technical, ethical, and business challenges. For leaders navigating AI's transformative landscape, this book serves as a strategic compass from concept to successful deployment.

— Sankaran Venkataramani, Partner, KPMG, India

Successful AI projects demand more than vision—they require methodologies that ensure intended and explainable outcomes. Jay and Alain have produced a practical, accessible guide covering the full AI project lifecycle with best practices, tools, and performance indicators. It bridges traditional requirements-driven development with the probabilistic nature of AI systems. A valuable reference for project leaders seeking to maximize the business, research, and ethical benefits of AI initiatives.

— Kevin Moran, Business & Technology Executive, Abaco Systems, HERE Technologies, Motorola, USA

www.ingramcontent.com/pod-product-compliance
Ingram Content Group UK Ltd.
Pitfield, Milton Keynes, MK11 3LW, UK
UKHW011513190726
13845UKWH00034B/1235

9 789334 419405